December

Week 52

MW00957378

○ 27. MONDAY

PRIORITIES

○ 28. TUESDAY

○ 29. WEDNESDAY

TO DO

○ 30. THURSDAY

○ 31. FRIDAY

○ 1. SATURDAY / 2. SUNDAY

January

Week 1

01/03/22 - 01/09/22

3. MONDAY

PRIORITIES

4. TUESDAY

5. WEDNESDAY

TO DO

6. THURSDAY

7. FRIDAY

8. SATURDAY / 9. SUNDAY

January

Week 2

01/10/22 - 01/16/22

○ 10. MONDAY

PRIORITIES

○ 11. TUESDAY

○ 12. WEDNESDAY

TO DO

○ 13. THURSDAY

○ 14. FRIDAY

○ 15. SATURDAY / 16. SUNDAY

January

Week 3

01/17/22 - 01/23/22

○ 17. MONDAY

PRIORITIES

○ 18. TUESDAY

○ 19. WEDNESDAY

TO DO

○ 20. THURSDAY

○ 21. FRIDAY

○ 22. SATURDAY / 23. SUNDAY

January

Week 4

01/24/22 - 01/30/22

○ 24. MONDAY

PRIORITIES

○ 25. TUESDAY

○ 26. WEDNESDAY

TO DO

○ 27. THURSDAY

○ 28. FRIDAY

○ 29. SATURDAY / 30. SUNDAY

January

Week 5

01/31/22 - 02/06/22

○ 31. MONDAY

PRIORITIES

○ 1. TUESDAY

○ 2. WEDNESDAY

TO DO

○ 3. THURSDAY

○ 4. FRIDAY

○ 5. SATURDAY / 6. SUNDAY

February

Week 6

02/07/22 - 02/13/22

○ 7. MONDAY

PRIORITIES

○ 8. TUESDAY

○ 9. WEDNESDAY

TO DO

○ 10. THURSDAY

○ 11. FRIDAY

○ 12. SATURDAY / 13. SUNDAY

February

Week 7

02/14/22 - 02/20/22

○ 14. MONDAY

PRIORITIES

○ 15. TUESDAY

○ 16. WEDNESDAY

TO DO

○ 17. THURSDAY

○ 18. FRIDAY

○ 19. SATURDAY / 20. SUNDAY

February

Week 8

02/21/22 - 02/27/22

○ 21. MONDAY

PRIORITIES

○ 22. TUESDAY

○ 23. WEDNESDAY

TO DO

○ 24. THURSDAY

○ 25. FRIDAY

○ 26. SATURDAY / 27. SUNDAY

February

Week 9

02/28/22 - 03/06/22

○ 28. MONDAY

PRIORITIES

○ 1. TUESDAY

○ 2. WEDNESDAY

TO DO

○ 3. THURSDAY

○ 4. FRIDAY

○ 5. SATURDAY / 6. SUNDAY

March

Week 10

03/07/22 - 03/13/22

○ 7. MONDAY

PRIORITIES

○ 8. TUESDAY

○ 9. WEDNESDAY

TO DO

○ 10. THURSDAY

○ 11. FRIDAY

○ 12. SATURDAY / 13. SUNDAY

March

Week 11

03/14/22 - 03/20/22

14. MONDAY

PRIORITIES

15. TUESDAY

16. WEDNESDAY

TO DO

17. THURSDAY

18. FRIDAY

19. SATURDAY / 20. SUNDAY

March

Week 12

03/21/22 - 03/27/22

○ 21. MONDAY

PRIORITIES

○ 22. TUESDAY

○ 23. WEDNESDAY

TO DO

○ 24. THURSDAY

○ 25. FRIDAY

○ 26. SATURDAY / 27. SUNDAY

March

Week 13

03/28/22 - 04/03/22

○ 28. MONDAY

PRIORITIES

○ 29. TUESDAY

○ 30. WEDNESDAY

TO DO

○ 31. THURSDAY

○ 1. FRIDAY

○ 2. SATURDAY / 3. SUNDAY

April

Week 14

04/04/22 - 04/10/22

4. MONDAY

PRIORITIES

5. TUESDAY

6. WEDNESDAY

TO DO

7. THURSDAY

8. FRIDAY

9. SATURDAY / 10. SUNDAY

April

Week 15

04/11/22 - 04/17/22

○ 11. MONDAY

PRIORITIES

○ 12. TUESDAY

○ 13. WEDNESDAY

TO DO

○ 14. THURSDAY

○ 15. FRIDAY

○ 16. SATURDAY / 17. SUNDAY

April

Week 16

04/18/22 - 04/24/22

○ 18. MONDAY

PRIORITIES

○ 19. TUESDAY

○ 20. WEDNESDAY

TO DO

○ 21. THURSDAY

○ 22. FRIDAY

○ 23. SATURDAY / 24. SUNDAY

April

Week 17

04/25/22 - 05/01/22

25. MONDAY

PRIORITIES

26. TUESDAY

27. WEDNESDAY

TO DO

28. THURSDAY

29. FRIDAY

30. SATURDAY / 1. SUNDAY

May

Week 18

05/02/22 - 05/08/22

○ 2. MONDAY

PRIORITIES

○ 3. TUESDAY

○ 4. WEDNESDAY

TO DO

○ 5. THURSDAY

○ 6. FRIDAY

○ 7. SATURDAY / 8. SUNDAY

May

Week 19

05/09/22 - 05/15/22

○ 9. MONDAY

PRIORITIES

○ 10. TUESDAY

○ 11. WEDNESDAY

TO DO

○ 12. THURSDAY

○ 13. FRIDAY

○ 14. SATURDAY / 15. SUNDAY

May

Week 20

05/16/22 - 05/22/22

16. MONDAY

PRIORITIES

17. TUESDAY

18. WEDNESDAY

TO DO

19. THURSDAY

20. FRIDAY

21. SATURDAY / 22. SUNDAY

May

Week 21

05/23/22 - 05/29/22

23. MONDAY

24. TUESDAY

25. WEDNESDAY

26. THURSDAY

27. FRIDAY

28. SATURDAY / 29. SUNDAY

PRIORITIES

TO DO

May

Week 22

05/30/22 - 06/05/22

○ 30. MONDAY

PRIORITIES

○ 31. TUESDAY

○ 1. WEDNESDAY

TO DO

○ 2. THURSDAY

○ 3. FRIDAY

○ 4. SATURDAY / 5. SUNDAY

June

Week 23

06/06/22 - 06/12/22

6. MONDAY

PRIORITIES

7. TUESDAY

8. WEDNESDAY

TO DO

9. THURSDAY

10. FRIDAY

11. SATURDAY / 12. SUNDAY

June

Week 24

06/13/22 - 06/19/22

13. MONDAY

PRIORITIES

14. TUESDAY

15. WEDNESDAY

TO DO

16. THURSDAY

17. FRIDAY

18. SATURDAY / 19. SUNDAY

June

Week 25

06/20/22 - 06/26/22

○ 20. MONDAY

PRIORITIES

○ 21. TUESDAY

○ 22. WEDNESDAY

TO DO

○ 23. THURSDAY

○ 24. FRIDAY

○ 25. SATURDAY / 26. SUNDAY

June

Week 26

06/27/22 - 07/03/22

○ 27. MONDAY

PRIORITIES

○ 28. TUESDAY

○ 29. WEDNESDAY

TO DO

○ 30. THURSDAY

○ 1. FRIDAY

○ 2. SATURDAY / 3. SUNDAY

July

Week 27

07/04/22 - 07/10/22

4. MONDAY

PRIORITIES

5. TUESDAY

6. WEDNESDAY

TO DO

7. THURSDAY

8. FRIDAY

9. SATURDAY / 10. SUNDAY

July

Week 28

07/11/22 - 07/17/22

11. MONDAY

PRIORITIES

12. TUESDAY

13. WEDNESDAY

TO DO

14. THURSDAY

15. FRIDAY

16. SATURDAY / 17. SUNDAY

July

Week 29

07/18/22 - 07/24/22

18. MONDAY

PRIORITIES

19. TUESDAY

20. WEDNESDAY

TO DO

21. THURSDAY

22. FRIDAY

23. SATURDAY / 24. SUNDAY

July

Week 30

07/25/22 - 07/31/22

25. MONDAY

PRIORITIES

26. TUESDAY

27. WEDNESDAY

TO DO

28. THURSDAY

29. FRIDAY

30. SATURDAY / 31. SUNDAY

August

Week 31

08/01/22 - 08/07/22

○ 1. MONDAY

PRIORITIES

○ 2. TUESDAY

○ 3. WEDNESDAY

TO DO

○ 4. THURSDAY

○ 5. FRIDAY

○ 6. SATURDAY / 7. SUNDAY

August

Week 32

08/08/22 - 08/14/22

○ 8. MONDAY

○ 9. TUESDAY

○ 10. WEDNESDAY

○ 11. THURSDAY

○ 12. FRIDAY

○ 13. SATURDAY / 14. SUNDAY

PRIORITIES

TO DO

August

Week 33

08/15/22 - 08/21/22

15. MONDAY

PRIORITIES

16. TUESDAY

17. WEDNESDAY

TO DO

18. THURSDAY

19. FRIDAY

20. SATURDAY / 21. SUNDAY

August

Week 34

08/22/22 - 08/28/22

○ 22. MONDAY

PRIORITIES

○ 23. TUESDAY

○ 24. WEDNESDAY

TO DO

○ 25. THURSDAY

○ 26. FRIDAY

○ 27. SATURDAY / 28. SUNDAY

August

Week 35

08/29/22 - 09/04/22

○ 29. MONDAY

PRIORITIES

○ 30. TUESDAY

○ 31. WEDNESDAY

TO DO

○ 1. THURSDAY

○ 2. FRIDAY

○ 3. SATURDAY / 4. SUNDAY

September

Week 36

09/05/22 - 09/11/22

○ 5. MONDAY

PRIORITIES

○ 6. TUESDAY

○ 7. WEDNESDAY

TO DO

○ 8. THURSDAY

○ 9. FRIDAY

○ 10. SATURDAY / 11. SUNDAY

September

Week 37

09/12/22 - 09/18/22

○ 12. MONDAY

PRIORITIES

○ 13. TUESDAY

○ 14. WEDNESDAY

TO DO

○ 15. THURSDAY

○ 16. FRIDAY

○ 17. SATURDAY / 18. SUNDAY

September

Week 38

09/19/22 - 09/25/22

○ 19. MONDAY

○ 20. TUESDAY

○ 21. WEDNESDAY

○ 22. THURSDAY

○ 23. FRIDAY

○ 24. SATURDAY / 25. SUNDAY

PRIORITIES

TO DO

September

Week 39

09/26/22 - 10/02/22

○ 26. MONDAY

○ 27. TUESDAY

○ 28. WEDNESDAY

○ 29. THURSDAY

○ 30. FRIDAY

○ 1. SATURDAY / 2. SUNDAY

PRIORITIES

TO DO

October

Week 40

10/03/22 - 10/09/22

3. MONDAY

PRIORITIES

4. TUESDAY

5. WEDNESDAY

TO DO

6. THURSDAY

7. FRIDAY

8. SATURDAY / 9. SUNDAY

October

Week 41

10/10/22 - 10/16/22

○ 10. MONDAY

PRIORITIES

○ 11. TUESDAY

○ 12. WEDNESDAY

TO DO

○ 13. THURSDAY

○ 14. FRIDAY

○ 15. SATURDAY / 16. SUNDAY

October

Week 42

10/17/22 - 10/23/22

○ 17. MONDAY

PRIORITIES

○ 18. TUESDAY

○ 19. WEDNESDAY

TO DO

○ 20. THURSDAY

○ 21. FRIDAY

○ 22. SATURDAY / 23. SUNDAY

October

Week 43

10/24/22 - 10/30/22

○ 24. MONDAY

○ 25. TUESDAY

○ 26. WEDNESDAY

○ 27. THURSDAY

○ 28. FRIDAY

○ 29. SATURDAY / 30. SUNDAY

PRIORITIES

TO DO

October

Week 44

10/31/22 - 11/06/22

31. MONDAY

PRIORITIES

1. TUESDAY

2. WEDNESDAY

TO DO

3. THURSDAY

4. FRIDAY

5. SATURDAY / 6. SUNDAY

November

Week 45

11/07/22 - 11/13/22

- [ ] 7. MONDAY

PRIORITIES

- [ ] 8. TUESDAY

- [ ] 9. WEDNESDAY

TO DO

- [ ] 10. THURSDAY

- [ ] 11. FRIDAY

- [ ] 12. SATURDAY / 13. SUNDAY

November

Week 46

11/14/22 - 11/20/22

14. MONDAY

15. TUESDAY

16. WEDNESDAY

17. THURSDAY

18. FRIDAY

19. SATURDAY / 20. SUNDAY

PRIORITIES

TO DO

November

Week 47

11/21/22 - 11/27/22

- ○ 21. MONDAY

PRIORITIES

- ○ 22. TUESDAY
- ○ 23. WEDNESDAY

TO DO

- ○ 24. THURSDAY
- ○ 25. FRIDAY
- ○ 26. SATURDAY / 27. SUNDAY

November

Week 48

11/28/22 - 12/04/22

28. MONDAY

PRIORITIES

29. TUESDAY

30. WEDNESDAY

TO DO

1. THURSDAY

2. FRIDAY

3. SATURDAY / 4. SUNDAY

December

Week 49

12/05/22 - 12/11/22

5. MONDAY

PRIORITIES

6. TUESDAY

7. WEDNESDAY

TO DO

8. THURSDAY

9. FRIDAY

10. SATURDAY / 11. SUNDAY

December

Week 50

12/12/22 - 12/18/22

○ 12. MONDAY

PRIORITIES

○ 13. TUESDAY

○ 14. WEDNESDAY

TO DO

○ 15. THURSDAY

○ 16. FRIDAY

○ 17. SATURDAY / 18. SUNDAY

December

Week 51

12/19/22 - 12/25/22

- ○ 19. MONDAY
- ○ 20. TUESDAY
- ○ 21. WEDNESDAY
- ○ 22. THURSDAY
- ○ 23. FRIDAY
- ○ 24. SATURDAY / 25. SUNDAY

PRIORITIES

TO DO

December

Week 52

12/26/22 - 01/01/23

○ 26. MONDAY

PRIORITIES

○ 27. TUESDAY

○ 28. WEDNESDAY

TO DO

○ 29. THURSDAY

○ 30. FRIDAY

○ 31. SATURDAY / 1. SUNDAY

January

Week 1

01/02/23 - 01/08/23

○ 2. MONDAY

PRIORITIES

○ 3. TUESDAY

○ 4. WEDNESDAY

TO DO

○ 5. THURSDAY

○ 6. FRIDAY

○ 7. SATURDAY / 8. SUNDAY

January

Week 2

01/09/23 - 01/15/23

9. MONDAY

10. TUESDAY

11. WEDNESDAY

12. THURSDAY

13. FRIDAY

14. SATURDAY / 15. SUNDAY

PRIORITIES

TO DO

January

Week 3

01/16/23 - 01/22/23

○ 16. MONDAY

○ 17. TUESDAY

○ 18. WEDNESDAY

○ 19. THURSDAY

○ 20. FRIDAY

○ 21. SATURDAY / 22. SUNDAY

PRIORITIES

TO DO

January

Week 4

01/23/23 - 01/29/23

○ 23. MONDAY

PRIORITIES

○ 24. TUESDAY

○ 25. WEDNESDAY

TO DO

○ 26. THURSDAY

○ 27. FRIDAY

○ 28. SATURDAY / 29. SUNDAY

January

Week 5

01/30/23 - 02/05/23

○ 30. MONDAY

PRIORITIES

○ 31. TUESDAY

○ 1. WEDNESDAY

TO DO

○ 2. THURSDAY

○ 3. FRIDAY

○ 4. SATURDAY / 5. SUNDAY

February

Week 6

02/06/23 - 02/12/23

○ 6. MONDAY

PRIORITIES

○ 7. TUESDAY

○ 8. WEDNESDAY

TO DO

○ 9. THURSDAY

○ 10. FRIDAY

○ 11. SATURDAY / 12. SUNDAY

February

Week 7

02/13/23 - 02/19/23

○ 13. MONDAY

PRIORITIES

○ 14. TUESDAY

○ 15. WEDNESDAY

TO DO

○ 16. THURSDAY

○ 17. FRIDAY

○ 18. SATURDAY / 19. SUNDAY

February

Week 8

02/20/23 - 02/26/23

- ○ 20. MONDAY
- ○ 21. TUESDAY
- ○ 22. WEDNESDAY
- ○ 23. THURSDAY
- ○ 24. FRIDAY
- ○ 25. SATURDAY / 26. SUNDAY

PRIORITIES

TO DO

February

Week 9

02/27/23 - 03/05/23

○ 27. MONDAY

PRIORITIES

○ 28. TUESDAY

○ 1. WEDNESDAY

TO DO

○ 2. THURSDAY

○ 3. FRIDAY

○ 4. SATURDAY / 5. SUNDAY

March

Week 10

03/06/23 - 03/12/23

○ 6. MONDAY

○ 7. TUESDAY

○ 8. WEDNESDAY

○ 9. THURSDAY

○ 10. FRIDAY

○ 11. SATURDAY / 12. SUNDAY

PRIORITIES

TO DO

March

Week 11

03/13/23 - 03/19/23

○ 13. MONDAY

PRIORITIES

○ 14. TUESDAY

○ 15. WEDNESDAY

TO DO

○ 16. THURSDAY

○ 17. FRIDAY

○ 18. SATURDAY / 19. SUNDAY

March

Week 12

03/20/23 - 03/26/23

○ 20. MONDAY

PRIORITIES

○ 21. TUESDAY

○ 22. WEDNESDAY

TO DO

○ 23. THURSDAY

○ 24. FRIDAY

○ 25. SATURDAY / 26. SUNDAY

March

Week 13

03/27/23 - 04/02/23

○ 27. MONDAY

PRIORITIES

○ 28. TUESDAY

○ 29. WEDNESDAY

TO DO

○ 30. THURSDAY

○ 31. FRIDAY

○ 1. SATURDAY / 2. SUNDAY

April

Week 14

04/03/23 - 04/09/23

○ 3. MONDAY

PRIORITIES

○ 4. TUESDAY

○ 5. WEDNESDAY

TO DO

○ 6. THURSDAY

○ 7. FRIDAY

○ 8. SATURDAY / 9. SUNDAY

April

Week 15

04/10/23 - 04/16/23

○ 10. MONDAY

PRIORITIES

○ 11. TUESDAY

○ 12. WEDNESDAY

TO DO

○ 13. THURSDAY

○ 14. FRIDAY

○ 15. SATURDAY / 16. SUNDAY

April

Week 16

04/17/23 - 04/23/23

○ 17. MONDAY

PRIORITIES

○ 18. TUESDAY

○ 19. WEDNESDAY

TO DO

○ 20. THURSDAY

○ 21. FRIDAY

○ 22. SATURDAY / 23. SUNDAY

April

Week 17

04/24/23 - 04/30/23

24. MONDAY

25. TUESDAY

26. WEDNESDAY

27. THURSDAY

28. FRIDAY

29. SATURDAY / 30. SUNDAY

PRIORITIES

TO DO

May

Week 18

05/01/23 - 05/07/23

○ 1. MONDAY

PRIORITIES

○ 2. TUESDAY

○ 3. WEDNESDAY

TO DO

○ 4. THURSDAY

○ 5. FRIDAY

○ 6. SATURDAY / 7. SUNDAY

May

Week 19

05/08/23 - 05/14/23

○ 8. MONDAY

○ 9. TUESDAY

○ 10. WEDNESDAY

○ 11. THURSDAY

○ 12. FRIDAY

○ 13. SATURDAY / 14. SUNDAY

PRIORITIES

TO DO

May

Week 20

05/15/23 - 05/21/23

○ 15. MONDAY

PRIORITIES

○ 16. TUESDAY

○ 17. WEDNESDAY

TO DO

○ 18. THURSDAY

○ 19. FRIDAY

○ 20. SATURDAY / 21. SUNDAY

May

Week 21

05/22/23 - 05/28/23

○ 22. MONDAY

PRIORITIES

○ 23. TUESDAY

○ 24. WEDNESDAY

TO DO

○ 25. THURSDAY

○ 26. FRIDAY

○ 27. SATURDAY / 28. SUNDAY

May

Week 22

05/29/23 - 06/04/23

○ 29. MONDAY

PRIORITIES

○ 30. TUESDAY

○ 31. WEDNESDAY

TO DO

○ 1. THURSDAY

○ 2. FRIDAY

○ 3. SATURDAY / 4. SUNDAY

June

Week 23

06/05/23 - 06/11/23

○ 5. MONDAY

PRIORITIES

○ 6. TUESDAY

○ 7. WEDNESDAY

TO DO

○ 8. THURSDAY

○ 9. FRIDAY

○ 10. SATURDAY / 11. SUNDAY

June

Week 24

06/12/23 - 06/18/23

12. MONDAY

13. TUESDAY

14. WEDNESDAY

15. THURSDAY

16. FRIDAY

17. SATURDAY / 18. SUNDAY

PRIORITIES

TO DO

June

Week 25

06/19/23 - 06/25/23

○ 19. MONDAY

PRIORITIES

○ 20. TUESDAY

○ 21. WEDNESDAY

TO DO

○ 22. THURSDAY

○ 23. FRIDAY

○ 24. SATURDAY / 25. SUNDAY

June

Week 26

06/26/23 - 07/02/23

○ 26. MONDAY

PRIORITIES

○ 27. TUESDAY

○ 28. WEDNESDAY

TO DO

○ 29. THURSDAY

○ 30. FRIDAY

○ 1. SATURDAY / 2. SUNDAY

July

Week 27

07/03/23 - 07/09/23

3. MONDAY

PRIORITIES

4. TUESDAY

5. WEDNESDAY

TO DO

6. THURSDAY

7. FRIDAY

8. SATURDAY / 9. SUNDAY

July

Week 28

07/10/23 - 07/16/23

○ 10. MONDAY

PRIORITIES

○ 11. TUESDAY

○ 12. WEDNESDAY

TO DO

○ 13. THURSDAY

○ 14. FRIDAY

○ 15. SATURDAY / 16. SUNDAY

July

Week 29

07/17/23 - 07/23/23

○ 17. MONDAY

PRIORITIES

○ 18. TUESDAY

○ 19. WEDNESDAY

TO DO

○ 20. THURSDAY

○ 21. FRIDAY

○ 22. SATURDAY / 23. SUNDAY

July

Week 30

07/24/23 - 07/30/23

24. MONDAY

PRIORITIES

25. TUESDAY

26. WEDNESDAY

TO DO

27. THURSDAY

28. FRIDAY

29. SATURDAY / 30. SUNDAY

July

Week 31

07/31/23 - 08/06/23

○ 31. MONDAY

PRIORITIES

○ 1. TUESDAY

○ 2. WEDNESDAY

TO DO

○ 3. THURSDAY

○ 4. FRIDAY

○ 5. SATURDAY / 6. SUNDAY

August

Week 32

08/07/23 - 08/13/23

○ 7. MONDAY

PRIORITIES

○ 8. TUESDAY

○ 9. WEDNESDAY

TO DO

○ 10. THURSDAY

○ 11. FRIDAY

○ 12. SATURDAY / 13. SUNDAY

August

Week 33

08/14/23 - 08/20/23

○ 14. MONDAY

PRIORITIES

○ 15. TUESDAY

○ 16. WEDNESDAY

TO DO

○ 17. THURSDAY

○ 18. FRIDAY

○ 19. SATURDAY / 20. SUNDAY

August

Week 34

08/21/23 - 08/27/23

○ 21. MONDAY

PRIORITIES

○ 22. TUESDAY

○ 23. WEDNESDAY

TO DO

○ 24. THURSDAY

○ 25. FRIDAY

○ 26. SATURDAY / 27. SUNDAY

August

Week 35

08/28/23 - 09/03/23

○ 28. MONDAY

PRIORITIES

○ 29. TUESDAY

○ 30. WEDNESDAY

TO DO

○ 31. THURSDAY

○ 1. FRIDAY

○ 2. SATURDAY / 3. SUNDAY

September

Week 36

09/04/23 - 09/10/23

○ 4. MONDAY

PRIORITIES

○ 5. TUESDAY

○ 6. WEDNESDAY

TO DO

○ 7. THURSDAY

○ 8. FRIDAY

○ 9. SATURDAY / 10. SUNDAY

September

Week 37

09/11/23 - 09/17/23

○ 11. MONDAY

PRIORITIES

○ 12. TUESDAY

○ 13. WEDNESDAY

TO DO

○ 14. THURSDAY

○ 15. FRIDAY

○ 16. SATURDAY / 17. SUNDAY

September

Week 38

09/18/23 - 09/24/23

18. MONDAY

19. TUESDAY

20. WEDNESDAY

21. THURSDAY

22. FRIDAY

23. SATURDAY / 24. SUNDAY

PRIORITIES

TO DO

September

Week 39

09/25/23 - 10/01/23

○ 25. MONDAY

PRIORITIES

○ 26. TUESDAY

○ 27. WEDNESDAY

TO DO

○ 28. THURSDAY

○ 29. FRIDAY

○ 30. SATURDAY / 1. SUNDAY

October

Week 40

10/02/23 - 10/08/23

○ 2. MONDAY

PRIORITIES

○ 3. TUESDAY

○ 4. WEDNESDAY

TO DO

○ 5. THURSDAY

○ 6. FRIDAY

○ 7. SATURDAY / 8. SUNDAY

October

Week 41

10/09/23 - 10/15/23

○ 9. MONDAY

PRIORITIES

○ 10. TUESDAY

○ 11. WEDNESDAY

TO DO

○ 12. THURSDAY

○ 13. FRIDAY

○ 14. SATURDAY / 15. SUNDAY

October

Week 42

10/16/23 - 10/22/23

○ 16. MONDAY

PRIORITIES

○ 17. TUESDAY

○ 18. WEDNESDAY

TO DO

○ 19. THURSDAY

○ 20. FRIDAY

○ 21. SATURDAY / 22. SUNDAY

October

Week 43

10/23/23 - 10/29/23

23. MONDAY

PRIORITIES

24. TUESDAY

25. WEDNESDAY

TO DO

26. THURSDAY

27. FRIDAY

28. SATURDAY / 29. SUNDAY

October

Week 44

10/30/23 - 11/05/23

○ 30. MONDAY

PRIORITIES

○ 31. TUESDAY

○ 1. WEDNESDAY

TO DO

○ 2. THURSDAY

○ 3. FRIDAY

○ 4. SATURDAY / 5. SUNDAY

November

Week 45

11/06/23 - 11/12/23

○ 6. MONDAY

PRIORITIES

○ 7. TUESDAY

○ 8. WEDNESDAY

TO DO

○ 9. THURSDAY

○ 10. FRIDAY

○ 11. SATURDAY / 12. SUNDAY

November

Week 46

11/13/23 - 11/19/23

○ 13. MONDAY

PRIORITIES

○ 14. TUESDAY

○ 15. WEDNESDAY

TO DO

○ 16. THURSDAY

○ 17. FRIDAY

○ 18. SATURDAY / 19. SUNDAY

November

Week 47

11/20/23 - 11/26/23

○ 20. MONDAY

PRIORITIES

○ 21. TUESDAY

○ 22. WEDNESDAY

TO DO

○ 23. THURSDAY

○ 24. FRIDAY

○ 25. SATURDAY / 26. SUNDAY

November

Week 48

11/27/23 - 12/03/23

○ 27. MONDAY

PRIORITIES

○ 28. TUESDAY

○ 29. WEDNESDAY

TO DO

○ 30. THURSDAY

○ 1. FRIDAY

○ 2. SATURDAY / 3. SUNDAY

December

Week 49

12/04/23 - 12/10/23

4. MONDAY

PRIORITIES

5. TUESDAY

6. WEDNESDAY

TO DO

7. THURSDAY

8. FRIDAY

9. SATURDAY / 10. SUNDAY

December

Week 50

12/11/23 - 12/17/23

- ○ 11. MONDAY
- ○ 12. TUESDAY
- ○ 13. WEDNESDAY
- ○ 14. THURSDAY
- ○ 15. FRIDAY
- ○ 16. SATURDAY / 17. SUNDAY

PRIORITIES

TO DO

December

Week 51

12/18/23 - 12/24/23

○ 18. MONDAY

PRIORITIES

○ 19. TUESDAY

○ 20. WEDNESDAY

TO DO

○ 21. THURSDAY

○ 22. FRIDAY

○ 23. SATURDAY / 24. SUNDAY

December

Week 52

12/25/23 - 12/31/23

○ 25. MONDAY

PRIORITIES

○ 26. TUESDAY

○ 27. WEDNESDAY

TO DO

○ 28. THURSDAY

○ 29. FRIDAY

○ 30. SATURDAY / 31. SUNDAY

Made in the USA
Monee, IL
08 March 2022

92489264R00059